THE MARINE MACHINE

the MARINE MACHINE

written and photographed by
WILLIAM MARES

DOUBLEDAY & COMPANY, INC.
GARDEN CITY, NEW YORK 1971

Library of Congress Catalog Card Number 70–131094
Copyright © 1970, 1971 by William Mares
All Rights Reserved
Printed in the United States of America
First Edition

FOREWORD

RECEIVE, degrade, sanitize, immunize, clothe, equip, train, pain, scold, mold, sand, and polish.

Young Americans are tedded into this Marine curing process by the drill instructor. His role is to be grossly misunderstood, much maligned, hated, cursed, until one night in faraway jungle foxholes, anticipating the landing of the next enemy mortar shell, many of these same recruits, grown to manhood during their first days of combat, mumble in reverence, "Thank God, Sergeant Jones was our DI at boot camp!"

Strange though it may be, this reverence will remain with them until death, whether in combat or in the relative calm of later civilian years.

With his words and pictures, William Mares produces for the reader an authentic description of how the Marine Corps chisels from the raw material it receives, the building blocks for its highly successful military machine. His unexcelled qualifications for doing so rest upon his unique experience of enduring recruit training as a "boot" and then, after he had left the Corps, his eleven-week observation of a recruit platoon from arrival to departure at Parris Island, South Carolina.

What is this "machine"? While the text but indirectly refers to it, the ultimate purpose of recruit training is to provide the material for the basic combat unit—the rifle squad. Through mud and guts and blood, frigid, torrid, rain, hail, the rifle squad must go. It must not fail. All the artillery, mortars, air support, tanks, communications, etc. have a single purpose—to help the rifle squad defeat the enemy. Even in a nuclear war, it will be the rifle squad, made up of former recruits such as these, that ultimately imposes our will on the enemy.

Little of recruit training teaches the techniques of destroying the enemy efficiently or economically. (That comes later.) Rather it emphasizes mental attitude and physical stamina. But besides the fundamentals of marksmanship, drill and physical training, the recruits learn three highly important things: (1) A proper respect for duly constituted authority (a lesson which must be learned sooner or later—better sooner, for the later it occurs, the more traumatic it may be). (2) How to take care of oneself (sanitation, care, and maintenance of clothing and equipment, etc.). (3) How to live with one's fellow men, a deep understanding of interdependence and the role it plays in successful combat.

Remember, it is not the natural human reaction to get up from a place of comparative safety and at the order of a sergeant or lieutenant, unhesitatingly go forward toward an armed and determined enemy whose purpose in life is to kill you. This is the very thing recruits are trained to do. Except for the will to win, there is little comparison between the training methods for this life-risking task and any other profession, avocation or game.

Marines, except at the Battle of Bull Run, have never been first away from the battlefield, and the training of recruits by dedicated, combat-experience DIs as described in this book, gets the credit.

Brutality or physical violence has never been condoned by the Marine Corps. When it is discovered, prompt investigation and disciplinary action has been taken by the proper authorities.

In support of the DIs who sometimes lay hands on recruits—they are like a mother or father who witnesses hours and days of exasperating actions and finally gives the kid a spanking, only to regret it later. They can be as proud of and as devoted to their recruits as any parent. The only difference is that they do their best not to show it.

Many DIs produce some of the best platoons without a single curse, a degrading remark, a brutal act, a laying-on of hands. Unbelievable but true. It can be done. But it isn't always. For human beings are dealing with human beings under the most trying, aggravating conditions and some inevitably fall below the standards of perfection.

The author aptly describes these trials and tribulations from the viewpoints of both recruit and DI. He tells it like it is, like it was, like it must be and like it's going to be until hopefully our Commanders-in-Chief no longer commit our young men to battles which they must win. Recruit training can then be pointed toward the Parade of Peace and not toward reducing the number in the Parade of Caskets.

DAVID M. SHOUP

CONTENTS

INTRODUCTION

THE MARINE CORPS has an unquestionable mystique. It is proud of its combat history and hides none of it under a basket. "Every Marine a rifleman," whether he greases planes, drives a truck, or carries a radio. No other service has such a plethora of nicknames: "Devildogs," "Leathernecks," "Gyrenes," "First to Fight." In an age of increasing technological specialization, some may question making the infantry an elite. The Marine Corps does not. Quite apolitical, they are the nearest thing to shock troops in the American military establishment.

Most Marines identify with the Corps and remain loyal long after their active duty ends. However, every Marine is *not* specifically a rifleman. Nor, even in wartime, does he necessarily serve in a combat zone. In part, the identification stems from the shared experience *in extremis* common to *all* enlisted Marines, be they six-months Reservists, enlistees, or thirty-year career men: Recruit Training, *BOOT CAMP!*

Young men join the Marine Corps for many reasons. They have dropped out of school; the draft is close on their heels; they had relatives in the Corps; they want to get away from their families; they want some kind of Instant Toughness; they are attracted by the recruiting posters and the recruiters' entreaties. For some it is a rejection of tradition; for others it is an enactment of America's ideals of heroism and valor.

I enlisted in the Marine Six-Month Program for more pedestrian reasons. I wanted to fulfill my military obligation as quickly as possible. It was peacetime and I was fascinated by the stories about Parris Island. Like everyone else who goes there, I regretted the decision as soon as I got off the bus. It seemed a world where scorn and ridicule were matters of course. Praise was unknown, friendships impossible, and, worst of all, we suffered collectively for individuals' mistakes.

During the next five years, I served as an undistinguished weekend Reservist, but I continued to think about the experience of boot camp. How did the Marine Corps begin to build its image? Was there method in the apparent madness which demeaned, degraded, and harassed all recruits uniformly? Did recruits become "Men" just by getting out of that place? Was "surviving" the training part of Parris Island's fascination?

What does boot camp look like through the eyes of a former recruit?

In May 1968, almost six years to the day since my own earlier Marine training, I drove back onto Parris Island. Outwardly, it was much the same. Some new barracks were under construction. The grounds were spotless, but the dust and sandfleas were still there. Platoons of recruits were being shepherded around by immaculate and unsmiling men in Smokey the Bear hats. Across the wide parade fields human figures and trees shimmered in the heat waves. In the evening above the sound of the crickets, I could hear the same mournful singsong cadence as a drill instructor marched his platoon back to the barracks.

But there were stark differences. The overriding one, of course, was the Vietnam war, killing four, five, six dozen Marines every week, boys who had left this place as recently as three months before. It was always a grim presence in the memories of the drill instructors and in the prospects of the recruits. Secondly, to fill the ranks of the discharged, wounded, and dead, the Marine Corps, like the other services, had been forced to reduce the length of training, increase the input of recruits and lower the mental and physical standards for enlistment. These changes have put increased pressure on the teacher-priest-guard-father-mother hen most responsible for training the recruits—the DIs.

The drill instructor, without question, continues to be the aspect of boot camp most remarked upon and most controversial.

For example, the average drill instructor addresses his recruits in language which is foul, extravagant, but after a time, meaningless. Cursing is routine and unemotional, just the reverse of what one normally associates with swearing. This is best illustrated by the universal use of the word "fuck" as noun, verb, adjective, gerund, past participle, even a syllable—"Outfucking-standing, Private Smith!"

Most of the notoriety about drill instructors, however, stems from something more serious than language. In 1956, a Sergeant McKeon took his platoon on an unauthorized march through a swamp near the rifle range. They got into water over their heads and in the resulting confusion, six recruits drowned. The consequent investigation was possibly the most wrenching internal crisis in the history of the Marine Corps. The entire training syllabus was revised and far closer supervision required. Therefore, the individual drill instructors had had nearly complete control over the training of recruits. What physical training (PT) they received came from him and there was often no distinction between punitive and constructive PT. He taught most of the academic subjects such as first aid, Marine Corps history, and sanitation and hygiene.

Now drill instructors must conform to a strict time schedule. Recruits must have seven and half hours of uninterrupted sleep. The SOP (Standard Operating Procedure for Recruit Training) explicitly prohibits touching recruits except for the purpose of "adjusting their posture." Only officers may administer "punishment." But drill instructors may give "extra instruction" to disobedient or recalcitrant recruits.

A few drill instructors still "thump" (strike) recruits and if caught, they are court-martialed. Almost all the drill instructors feel pressured by conditions not of their making. They believe that occasional corporal punishment or the threat of it is necessary to instill the discipline and toughness needed in combat. "How can we repair *verbally* in ten weeks eighteen years of parental indulgence? The officers only care if the recruits march in step and get to dental appointments on time. Should an NCO in combat have to *ask* his men to carry out orders?" They talk wistfully about their experience in boot camp, about how much tougher it was—it seems that even the Marine Corps has conflicts between generations.

In fact, the drill instructors themselves have changed. Ten to fifteen years ago, most had volunteered for Parris Island duty. They were single. Their life *was* the Marine Corps. They scorned recruits as "Kremlin agents sent to fuck up 'our' Marine Corps." Although most are still career Marines, many are now family men, "gorillas by day, lambs at night." On the whole, they are younger, and almost none volunteered to become drill instructors. Ninety-five percent are combat veterans.

For nearly ten weeks, ten-twelve hours a day, I watched three of these men (average age twenty-seven) take a seventy-five-man platoon through training. The only restriction was that I talk to no recruits.

As I worked I began to think of other situations in which people suffered similarly extreme changes in their freedom of action. Prisons, mental institutions, POW camps, and boarding schools came to mind. But it seemed that the closest analogy to boot camp was, paradoxically, a monastery.

Both institutions are based upon massive regimentation, denial, and a certain amount of degradation. They are isolated societies where humiliation is a principle means of control. But both have an avowedly *positive* end. They want to *convert* the recruit and novice. They want to give each a new collective identity. The religious order wants unquestioning obedience, the better to serve God. The Marine Corps, too, wants more than just "bodies." It wants more than mere acquiescence. It wants positive affirmation of orders, the better to perform and survive in battle. Thus discipline is defined as "instant willing obedience to orders." Such obedience, obviously, does not come instantly or painlessly.

The fact that the vast majority of recruits have volunteered is, in the Marine Corps' eyes, a major precondition for conversion. The

xiii

recruits have expressed the desire, however imperfectly understood, or thought out, to become "members of the World's Finest Fighting Organization." No matter how painful the training or how demeaning their treatment, the recruits hear a constant refrain from the drill instructor: "No one forced you to join. If you don't like it, then tough shit, sorry about that. You're here anyway."

During the ten weeks of boot camp, enlistment will almost seem like the last act of free will.

PREFACE

VERY FEW books spring fully conceived from the author's mind and this one is no exception. One evening, after my Marine service was over and largely forgotten, I was reading John Sack's book *M*, in which he followed an Army company through basic training to its first engagement in Vietnam.

It was really mind-boggling. Suddenly, I saw my own training in an entirely different light. When I had gone to Parris Island, it had been on something of a lark. There was no war. It was get in and get out. Sack's book, on the other hand, showed a profound and desolate connection between the training and potential death. Then it occurred to me—why not a photographic book doing the same thing with the Marines? I waited several weeks to make sure the idea was no penny vision. When it refused to go away, I outlined a proposal to officers at Marine Corps Headquarters.

They were receptive. However, they said it would be impossible for me to remain with a platoon of recruits all the way to Vietnam simply because the platoon itself would be split up. After leaving boot camp and then Infantry Training Regiment, individual Marines would receive more training according to their military occupation specialty: communications, artillery, tanks, etc. Most would indeed get to Vietnam but not as members of their original platoon. I decided, therefore, to concentrate on boot camp as an institution in itself and on those ten weeks as the first step in converting civilians into Marine riflemen.

The Marine Corps gave me carte blanche to follow one platoon through its entire training cycle, seven days a week, twenty-four hours a day, if I liked. The only restrictions were that I not talk with the recruits, nor could I sleep in the barracks. The recruits were told nothing about my work, only that they should ignore me. Given the state of shock in which most recruits find themselves, this was easy "advice" to follow.

My non-official status gave me a freedom of movement around the recruits neither enjoyed nor sought by the DIs. To balance my inevitable bias in favor of the recruits I tried to join the DIs for at least one meal a day to get some sense of *their* feelings and gripes.

I had originally planned to let the pictures tell the whole story, but then decided to write an accompanying text when I saw (and heard) more and more which was simply not susceptible of purely graphic treatment.

Of the myriad persons who gave me encouragement and help, four particular devil's advocates deserve mention. As sociologist, novelist, and journalist respectively, Tony Platt, Melinda Benton, and Guy Halverson read all or part of the manuscript and made invaluable comments from three quite different viewpoints. And John Tweedle, my first photographic mentor, helped me reduce over six thousand negatives to the 130 we finally used in the book.

Finally, a special note of thanks to Lieutenant Colonel Patrick Ryan, whose enthusiastic competition on the tennis courts, provided about the only breaks, other than reading during those ten weeks at Parris Island.

Chicago
September 1970

receiving

CHAPTER ONE

ALL DAY and night six days a week the buses rolled through the South Carolina lowlands carrying their consignments of recruits toward Parris Island. Along the way, their fresh-faced passengers swapped stories, cigarettes, and comfort. Almost before they knew it, the buses had squirted past a gate marked U. S. MARINE CORPS RECRUIT DEPOT, PARRIS ISLAND, SOUTH CAROLINA. Conversations tailed off as they rode down a long causeway lined with orderly oleanders. Once over a tidal stream, they were on the "Island." They caught brief glimpses of barracks and troops through the palm and oak trees before the buses stopped in front of a nondescript white building.

A sergeant came out and while the recruits eyed him curiously, he chatted with the bus driver. Suddenly he turned on them with crisp guttural scorn, **"*Shut your goddam mouths!* This is Receiving Barracks. I'm giving you assholes thirty seconds to get yourselves and all your shit off this bus and into that barracks. *Move!*"** Like flushed quail, they cascaded off the bus and into a starkly furnished room where they lined up at numbered positions.

From the Marine Corps' standpoint, the first hours and days at boot camp are the most important in terms of establishing a "psyche," that is, for making the recruits positively amenable to the training schedule, methods, and expectations. Although the Marine Corps denies any design, many buses arrive at night. Such nocturnal dumpings must make the transition more abrupt. The last batch of recruits may get only two or three hours sleep. In a word, the recruits are put in a modified state of shock.

A voice broke the uneasy silence:

YouarenowatRecruitReceivingBarracksMarineCorpsRecruit DepotParrisIslandSouthCarolinaThisisyourfirststepin becomingamemberoftheWorldsFinestFightingOrganization theUnitedStatesMarineCorpsYouwillbeinthecustodyofthis barracksforaperiodofapproximately12to24hoursDuring thattimeyouwillbeprocessedandformedintoarecruitplatoon. Afterthatyouwillbepickedupbyateamofdrillinstructors whowilltrainyouforthenexttenweeks.Throughoutyourtraining youshouldalwaysbealerttodowhatyouaretoldwhenyouaretold andtospeakonlywhenspokento. BeingprivatesintheMarineCorpsyouarethelowestofthelow andyouwillconductyourselvesaccordinglyaffordingall militarysuperiorspropermilitarycourtesyatalltimes.You willspeakonlywhenspokentoalwaysusingtheword"sir." IS THAT CLEAR RECRUITS? . . .

"Yes sir!" he made them scream until the sound they made was a sort of croak-bellow. He sneered and returned to his paperwork. The recruits tried to stand at attention. Like willows, they swayed gently. Insects buzzed and whirred against the fluorescent lights. Drops of sweat began maddening journeys down their staring faces. Before their furtively rotating eyeballs were written on posts injunctions like MORALE, TACT, COURAGE, and GUNG-HO.

Without warning, the drill instructor jumped out of his chair, grabbed a wastebasket labeled CONTRABAND and began a mass shakedown. The list of prohibited items was long. Obviously, the recruits could not have weapons, drugs, or pornography. Wallets and wedding rings they could keep but everything else from good luck charms to gum and deodorant had to go home or was dropped noisily into the

4

wastebasket. It was a systematic divestiture of the material expressions of individual taste. The drill instructor carried out this denuding task with dispatch except for occasional mocking references to the contents of personality laid out before him. "You come down here with this blade to cut me, fuckface? *Try it!*" One recruit had a pilot's training manual in his kit. "What the fuck you want to fly for? You queer, boy? . . . Ah, sweetie, did your mommy pack those pajamas for you with her own loving hands? *Send 'em home!*"

With little delay and even less ceremony, the recruits were lined up for a more graphic act of dispossession. A barber was on duty twenty-four hours a day to shear off their proud locks. Every thirty seconds, a bald recruit skittered out of the chair and down the hall for ID portraits. In an hour the barber stood ankle deep in brown, black, blond, and red sacrifice. For the recruits, it hardly sufficed that having no hair was sanitary, that it was military. It was an amputation, a malicious, offhand obliteration of the last means of expressing their individuality.

After being fingerprinted, blood-typed, and fitted for gas masks, the recruits were herded upstairs and left alone. "You pigs had *best* sleep!" Unguarded, they began to skylark. The duty drill instructor came storming back. "So, as soon as my back is turned, you want to fuck off?" He made them shout *"No sir!"* over and over again, before permitting them to go to sleep.

Reveille, the starkest of moments, seemed to come only minutes later. The relentless fluorescents went on. A trash can crashed in the middle of the room. Some madman beat on the top and a voice burst from the door *"Getupgetupgetupgetupgetup-you-scummy-pigs!"* Wild-eyed and sleep-sodden, the recruits clambered from their racks.

Not all the recruits were in the desired "state of shock" at this point. One with the build of a football player did not move fast enough to satisfy the drill instructor, who launched an abrasive, threatening harangue which grew in intensity as the recruit replied each time with an insinuating slurred, "Yesssirrrr!" The confrontation was a standoff, because the drill instructor had to return to the first floor to process more recruits.

The remaining hours of their stay at Receiving were relatively quiet. They drew uniforms, soap, towels, and cigarettes. There were notebooks filled with military information, and toothpaste, razors ("Everyone *will* shave!"), etc. Their civilian clothes and effects went into paper bags to be sent home.

In the late morning heat, they shifted nervously in their new uniforms and waited "at the position of attention" for their own drill instructors. Platoon 360 was about to come into ferocious being.

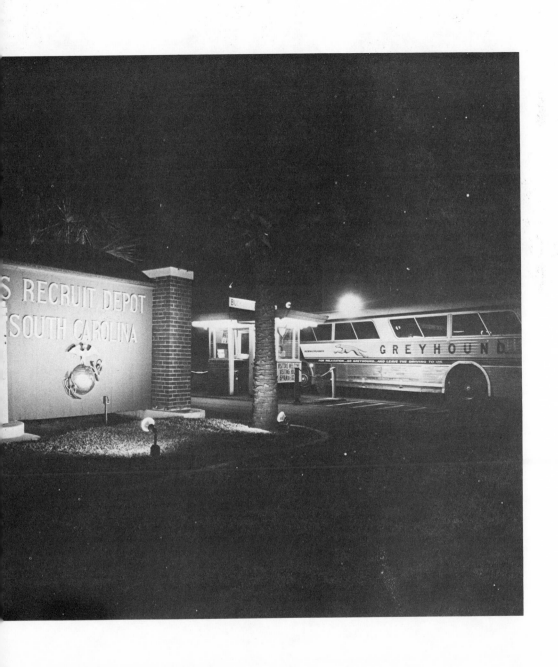

"Get your ass off that bus!"

"You sorry hunk of crap!
Why did *you* join the
Marine Corps?"

10

A list of articles
which recruits may *not*
keep in their possession.

WING IN YOUR POSSESSION
PHOTOGRAPHS LARGER THAN BILLFOLD SIZE
AND ANY FRAMED PICTURES.
PULP MAGAZINES OR BOOKS.
VALUABLE DOCUMENTS.
CHEWING GUM, CHEWING TOBACCO, OR ANY
PERISHABLE FOOD PRODUCTS.
JEWELRY AND CLOCKS OTHER THAN WATCHES
OR SIMPLE RINGS.
SHOE POLISH.
CAMERAS AND RADIOS.
WILL BE R
SENT HOME

It includes almost everything except wedding rings.

DI mocks recruit for having brought a pocket knife.
"Down here, you won't need anything except your ears
and a prayer book."

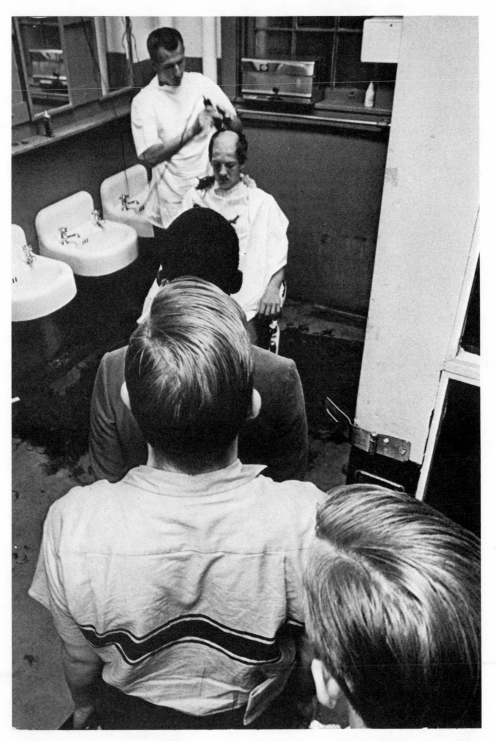

Line-up for haircuts.

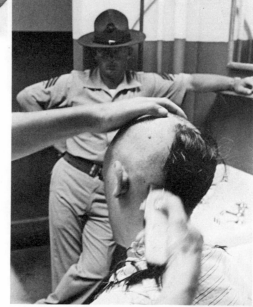

14   Cranial amputation.

A half-hour's work by the barber.
The hair of perhaps twenty recruits lies here.

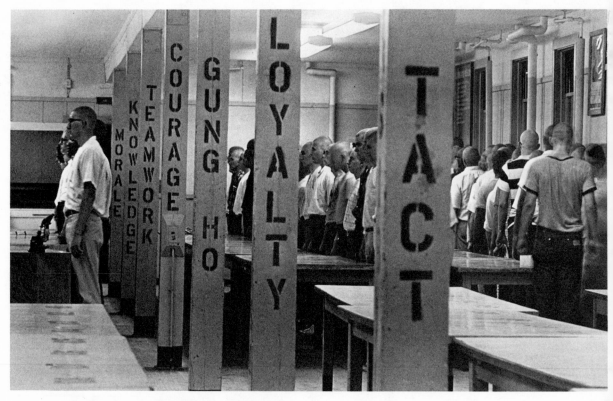

Standing, standing, standing.

18   **More standing, at 4:30 A.M. waiting outside in the moon's light, to be marched to chow.**

ID portrait.

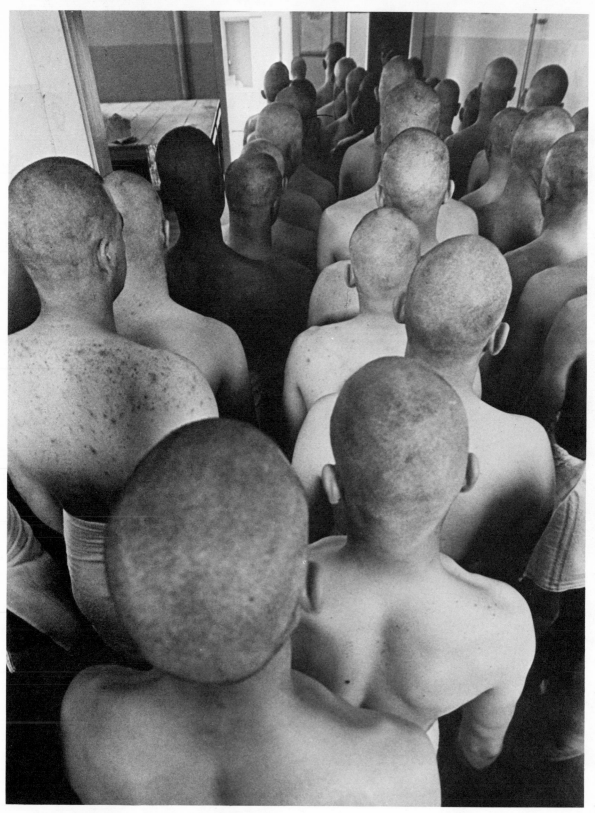

Stripped, these recruits are about to enter the Marine maw for clothing.

Waiting for clothes to cover their nakedness.

Ready (?)
for the beginning
of training.

forming

CHAPTER TWO

IN EVERY sense of the word, the week of Forming is a period of adjustment. The Marine Corps sets out to diminish and exorcise all civilian patterns of behavior. They assail the privates for thinking and acting for themselves. They offer mocking synonyms for the new military jargon: "Make a head call means 'tee-tee,' girls." They make individuality and physical oddities objects of derision by assigning nicknames such as Fat Albert, Boris Karloff, and King Kong. They punish just those actions which in civilian society seem the most automatic and innocent: "running your mouth," scratching, "eyeballing."

At the same time, the drill instructors begin to implant in the recruits a new constellation of habits and references. Use of the word "sir" should become a reflex action as should standing "at the position of attention." The endless shouting, staring, singing, and chanting force the recruits to concentrate their attention on the platoon's object: unity. The recruits should *begin* to think that "what's good for the platoon is good for me."

"There are three ways of doing anything, the right way, the wrong way, and the Marine Corps way. You *will* do everything the Marine Corps way. You've got one minute to get your worthless bodies outside and lined up on the painted footprints! *Move!*" As the seventy-five recruits tumbled out the door more drill instructors surrounded them. "Get your fucking feet on the paint! Both feet, dum-dum! Get over here, shitforbrains! You tired already? Move out, mob!"

They stumbled off, the drill instructors yelling, rhythmically but incomprehensibly: "Leh ri leh, ado leh ri leh, ado leh, leh ri leh . . ." Even when recruit ears began to hear "Left, Right, Left, Right!", their feet remained deaf. Those who had recovered from the initial state of shock at Receiving were pummeled back into it by the glare, noise and their bouncing sea bags. The drill instructors seemed to hurry the lead of the column so the rear would have to run. "Step off with a full 30-inch step. Your military left, assholes!" It was utterly bewildering. Every false step, every twitch, every gasp seemed to invite a verbal cuff. Along the half-mile distance to the 3rd Battalion area, the drill instructors halted the platoon for a rest, but made it clear that only "pussies" needed such a respite. Their first meal was scarcely less traumatic. Hardly anyone finished in the allotted twenty minutes, and one recruit was so frightened he vomited.

The next few days under the scorching sun merged into a confusion of shouts, steps, sweat, and lines. Lines for shots, lines for sheets, lines for chow, lines for mail. Whenever and wherever the platoon halted, it was at the position of attention. "At ease!" was a command unknown. Even the chowline was "asshole to bellybutton" and after each 6-inch step forward, they "locked their heels." Attempts to blow away the exasperating and relentless fleas were futile. And woe to the private caught batting at these tiny tormentors. Out of nowhere, a DI would crash through the ranks and scream: "Let my bugs eat, turd!"

The recruits learned to live from moment to uncertain moment. That togetherness as a prime virtue was apparent; that it was attainable to the satisfaction of the drill instructors was at best problematic. Everyone on the Island except other recruits seemed at best bored and at worst offended by their presence. They were indeed the "lowest of the low."

For long hours in the barracks, they learned how to salute, how to make their racks, how to mark clothing . . .

"Get your locker boxes, buckets, skivvie shirts and marking kits.

26

And if any of you pigs spill this ink, you better give your heart to God, because I've got your ass.

"From your marking kits, pull out the bottle of black, I repeat, *black* ink. With the thumb and index finger of your left hand, grasp the bottle firmly. Now take the thumb and index finger of your right hand and grasp the metal top of the bottle. Rotate the top slowly but firmly in a counterclockwise direction . . . *Goddammit!* That broken bottle will cost you, hog!"

The platoon drew more equipment, the most important being a rifle, their proclaimed *raison d'etre*. "If there is ever a question of caring for your rifle or your own scuzzy self, you had *best* choose the rifle!" They also took a battery of aptitude and IQ tests. Medical and dental exams filled another two days.

In the midst of these frenetic comings and goings, one private announced that he was a "CO" (conscientious objector). He could not define it but he knew he wanted out. Possibly thinking this a successful gambit, another private pleaded the Fifth Amendment when asked why he had been talking in the chowline. Neither succeeded and after talks with another kind of CO both found themselves increasingly chosen for extra duty.

The time came when the drill instructors felt that sterner treatment than verbal admonishment was required to discipline the recruits. However, the first time a drill instructor used it on Platoon 360, it backfired. "So you pigs want to fuck off when we aren't looking. Bends and thrusts, ready, begin!" They stared at him blankly. "Sir, what's a bend and thrust?"

At all times, the recruits had to carry with them small red notebooks filled with military information for which they were responsible. In fact, they almost never studied the contents except prior to exams. It didn't seem to matter to the drill instructors. Content was secondary to form. If the recruits had their noses buried in the notebooks, they couldn't "eyeball the area" or "run their mouths." Such a stance also helped cultivate the visual aspect of "attention," a "thousand-yard stare in a ten-foot room."

After the medical exams, the doctors certified several recruits as overweight. They became "fatbodies" with all the humiliations that name connotes. They were weighed thrice weekly, placed last in the chowline and had their food checked by a drill instructor. "I don't trust that hog," one said to his fellows as he rummaged through the recruit's lettuce. "He steals cookies."

One day a recruit approached a drill instructor. "Sir, I wonder if you . . ." "Did you hear anything, Sergeant Mathews? That scumbag couldn't have been talking to us. Or were you, you miserable piece of shit? Get this straight, sweetpea. An eye is something to look through. Point to it. Harder! A ewe is a female sheep. Do we look like female sheep? Until you get off this Island, you are 'the private.' There are many like you, but not many so humble. Get out of my sight!"

The only instance when recruits do not refer to themselves or anyone else in the third person is in the "Dialogue" which echoes through the squadbay each night after Taps:

I AM A UNITED STATES MARINE CORPS RECRUIT.
I SERVE IN THE FORCES WHICH GUARD MY COUNTRY
AND OUR WAY OF LIFE.
I AM PREPARED TO GIVE MY LIFE IN THEIR DEFENSE.
SO HELP ME GOD.
     GUNG-HO!   GUNG-HO!   GUNG-HO!
GOD BLESS ALL MARINES WHEREVER THEY ARE!

This is followed by the Lord's Prayer.

Despite the universally proclaimed incompetence and stupidity of all recruits, drill instructors choose a few recruits for positions of modest formal and informal responsibility within the platoon. The most physically imposing usually becomes the bearer of the platoon guidon. Two recruits are designated "scribes" and help maintain the platoon records. Four others become file leaders. But the most important job, in the DI's eyes, is that of "house mouse." His formal duty is to care for the "house," a cubicle with bathroom where the drill instructor on duty stays. Chosen for his small size, he becomes a sort of mascot and the butt of much mock harassment.

Without coffee and cigarettes, most drill instructors are more irritable than usual. Thus, replenishment of the DI's coffee cup or jug is a crucial job for the mouse. Platoon 360's mouse did not fare well on his first try. The senior drill instructor took one sip and spat out, "Mouse, the coffee's cold! You're a Kremlin spy sent here to fuck up my stomach!"

Such joking was as close to empathy as the DIs ever got. When a recruit thanked a DI for helping him repair a rifle sling, the DI hissed, "Don't thank me, hog. The government does it twice a month. You want to take over their job?" And when a recruit came to the drill instructors in tears because he could not memorize the General Orders of Interior Guard, they listened stonily, gave him permission to repeat them to another private but added, "We had *best* not catch you fucking off."

Each day contained a discretionary period known as "Commander's Time." Commonly, the drill instructors used these small chunks of time to teach drill or the manual of arms. Over and over again, they forced the recruits to repeat a single movement. "When you bring those rifles to Port Arms, I want to hear one *pop!* . . . Do it again, assholes!" Worst of all, the drill instructors loved to raze their very frustration: "Oh my. Are you girls mad? Well, then, stomp your feet!"

Praise, in the first weeks, was not grudging; it was nonexistent.

What the recruits cannot see is that Forming is also a period of adjustment for DIs. In each platoon, the senior drill instructor usually has had more experience than the juniors. An unwritten division of labor has developed between them. The juniors take the role of bad guys, "kicking ass and taking names," in DI parlance. The senior becomes something of a father figure, less given to punishment and rage. His technique is more verbal than physical. This divided responsibility is not utterly fixed. Sometimes, they reverse the roles, just to keep the recruits off balance.

In the very nature of their job, the DIs are perpetually on stage. They are models *par excellence.* In dress, deportment, and demeanor, they should convey the impression of the ideal NCO. As they evaluate the recruits, they themselves are being evaluated.

It takes a special kind of NCO to be able to stay on the recruits' asses hour after hour, day after day. It's a lot easier to make mistakes in another job. Here you hold yourself up to the recruits as a piece of perfection. They know when you fuck up. Make enough mistakes, and you have your own credibility gap.

The platoon's first hint that the DIs might have a trace of humanity came at the end of Forming. They called a "school circle" but instead of lecturing, they talked to the recruits informally.

"You have been here for about a week and you now have some impression of what we are looking for. You are only seventy-five of the millions who have come through this place. If you ever think you can't make it, that tomorrow cannot possibly be worse than yesterday, I've got news for you. It will, but that belief will keep you going.

"You are a member of Platoon 360. You will carry that with you for the rest of your life. While you are down here, you will have no higher loyalty. Your privacy begins and ends with the mail. But it is also *our* platoon. When you leave this Island, you take part of us with you. It's up to you how much.

"As a platoon, there are a number of awards you can win. These awards will be in the form of streamers attached to the guidon. White means all you maggots passed the Phase I exam. There are streamers for markmanship, drill competition, the obstacle course, and so on. If you hogs win seven streamers, you become a Superior Platoon. If you are as worthless as you seem so far, you will be a purple mob. The purple streamer goes for 90 percent participation in the Savings Bond drive and only Communists don't buy bonds. Any questions?"

"Sir, will most of the privates be going to Vietnam?"

"I haven't heard of any who haven't been there. Once you get there, the trial and error game is over. Forget what you're doing and I guaranfuckintee you, you'll get blown away. It's plain outright facts. Your job is to kill.

"Not all of you who go to Vietnam will come back but everyone has the same chance. You've got about three to four months before you get there. There is no time to dilly-dally in any phase of training. Fall asleep in one of these classes and you are endangering someone else's life. So wake the fuck up! Any more questions?"

30

One private rose shyly from the clustered bodies and almost whispered, "Sir, the private's feet hurt."

The DI looked at his boots, made a frantic effort to suppress a laugh, fixed a gruff expression on his face and said, "Of course they do, you stupid sonofabitch. The boots are on the wrong feet!"

"Welcome, scum!"

DI makes sure recruit
gets through the hatch
on the double.

32

Racing out of Receiving barracks and lining up on printed footprints.

Two DIs lose no time
in dressing down an
errant recruit.

"Everything by the numbers.
Alternate recruits will place
their locker boxes on the
lower bunk."

"You look around one more
time, maggot, and I'll give
you something to look at!"

One of the innumerable lines, this one for blood samples . . .

. . . and this one for X rays.

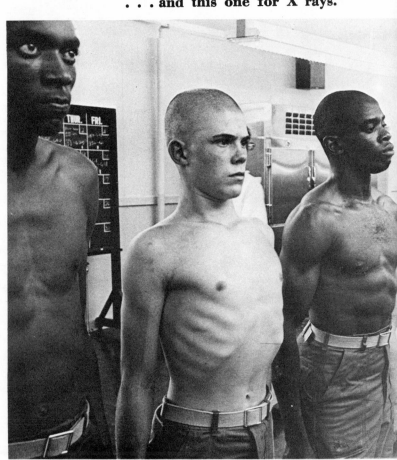

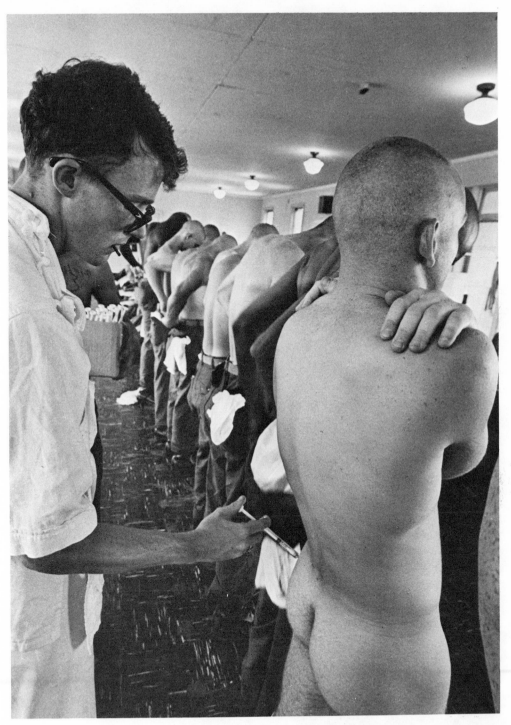

Gamma globulin shots are administered posteriorly.

A christening of sorts—
a fitting for barracks caps.

Rifle issue.

Another line,
this one for 782 gear
(tent, poncho, mess kit, etc.)

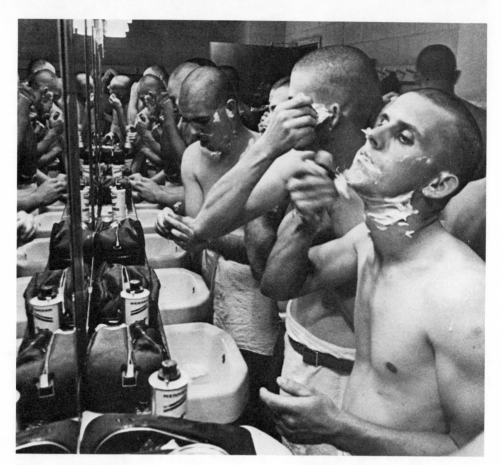

First shave.

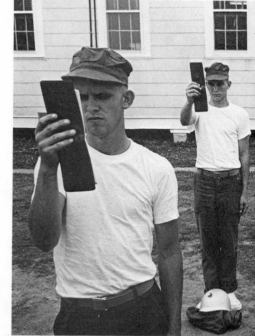

Recruits are never without
their red notebooks
and they study them in a
characteristic fashion.

Everything is pitched to the
lowest common intelligence.
Even tying bootlaces is a
subject and some take longer
than others to master it.

In the heat and newness
of the first days,
it is not uncommon for
a recruit to forget
left from right.

44

"Dress right, dress!"

Sunday is laundry day.

**Their first punishment—
bends and thrusts.**

**Individual punishment—
more bends and thrusts.**

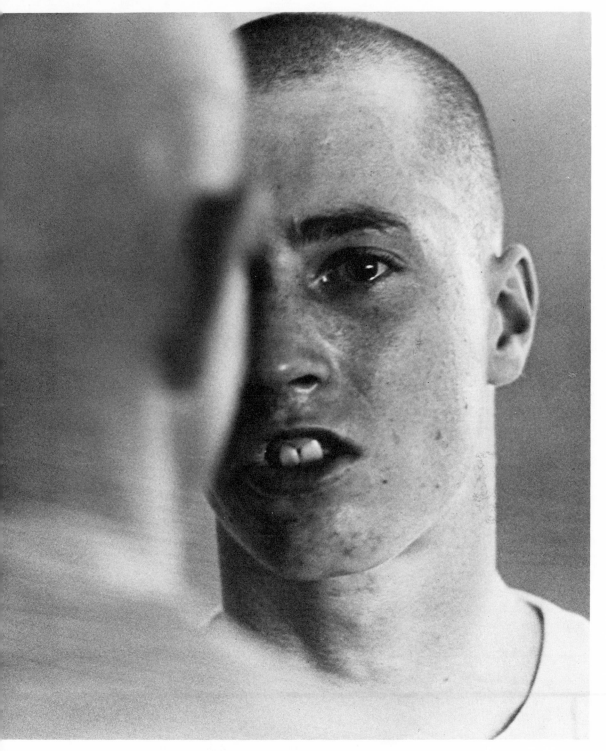

"But sir, the private *can't* remember his General Orders!"

One of the first classes in the squad bay,
an introduction to their *raison d'etre*, the rifle.

In the beginning was
the left foot.

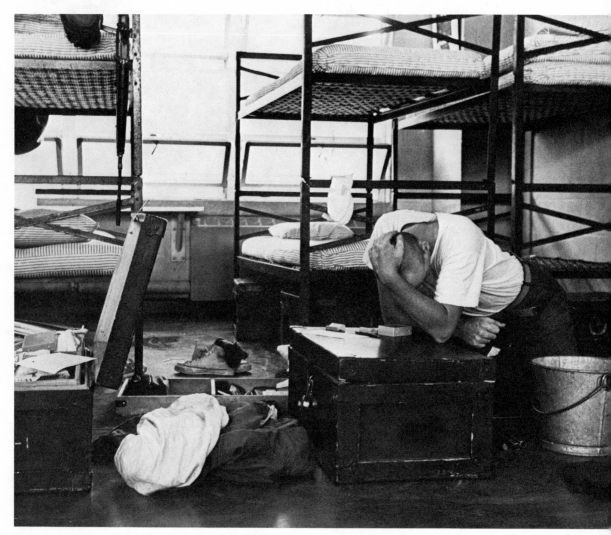

One private's private moment.

phase I

CHAPTER THREE

"ToGEther, ToGEther, get it together, girls!"

Whether they were marching, doing calisthenics, repeating the General Orders or standing at attention, Platoon 360 spent the first three weeks of formal training painfully learning the importance of collective discipline.

Scorn and ridicule remained part of their daily bread.

But there was a gradual shift from the proclaimed "worthlessness" of recruits as individuals to the "worthlessness" of the platoon as a whole. Unity was not enough. The drill instructors now sought unanimity.

The recruits became aware that they were part of a four platoon series. This configuration was designed to facilitate handling and to foster a competitive, indeed a combative spirit. Depending upon what lesson they sought to impart to the recruits, the DIs used the other platoon's performance as goads or strictures: "Look at those hogs in [Platoon] 362, fucking off as soon as their drill instructors' backs are turned. Are you that disloyal?"

The daily schedule during Phase I began and ended with PT. During those sessions, the air above Parris Island was filled with the sustained yelling of hundreds of recruits. The PT instructor contolled their voices as he controlled their sweating bodies. "If you pigs

53

want to sound off, we'll go back to push-ups. *I've* got all day." Many recruits were not in good physical shape and had difficulty with even the modest initial exercises. The platoon drill instructors moved among the recruits ferreting out those who seemed to be lagging. "Build men from you mountains of crap? The recruiter who signed you up must have been drunk!" But gradually the recruits *did* improve, though, of course, no one gave them credit for it.

After abbreviated showers had washed away some of the dirt and sweat, the platoon marched to a variety of formal classes in the mid-day hours. This "academic" side of boot camp included "First Aid," "Sanitation and Hygiene," "Military Customs and Courtesies," "Packs," "Weapons Familiarization," and "Marine Corps History." The last class was a sort of institutionalized myth-making. The instructor larded his lessons with disparaging remarks about the other services, while recounting episodes of Marine glory and tradition.

> During the battle of Belleau Wood in the First World War, one battalion of Marines had to take Hill ※142. It was heavily out-numbered but it had one thing going for it against all those Germans—something we are known for—Marksmanship! Marine privates like you were picking off Germans at 600 yards . . .
>
> The doggies don't have any history classes in basic training because they don't have any history . . .

The DIs gave some of the classes in the barracks. They deviated more from the lesson plans and used saltier exegeses than the other instructors:

> To fight you've got to be healthy. It'll surprise you how many diseases are carried by that little bastard that just flew by (pointing to a housefly) . . .
>
> Lice live on blood and when deprived of food, they die—no chance of them living on you anemic scum . . .
>
> Use common sense. If a scorpion bites a private, don't have him double-time to sickbay!

54

The training syllabus called for eight hours of bayonet instructions during Phase I. The main purpose was to teach aggressiveness. To this end, the recruits, armed with helmets and "pugilsticks," were urged to take out their frustrations on each other.

With four drill instructors and 150 other recruits watching, the two combatants could not reach a separate peace. Timidity's reward was another round. Informal intra-series competitions developed. The DIs kept score and loudly favored their own privates. The finale came when the seniors pitted their mice against one another. The diminutive recruits almost disappeared in the hot swirling, choking dust. Platoon 360's mouse won and was borne off the field of battle on the senior's shoulder, to the platoon's obvious enjoyment.

The screws of control, loosened slightly during pugilsticking, were tightened again on the obstacle courses. When one recruit could not lift himself over a barrier, a DI was there to hiss, "Come on, pussy, You gonna write home to Rosie tonight and tell how you conquered the O course today?"

One morning the DIs ordered Platoon 360 out of its barracks to stand the first of what would be a series of increasingly severe inspections. But none would gouge their senses and balance as this one did. First of all, the recruits had no idea of what was expected of them. Second, the inspectors were unfamiliar DIs. Third, there seemed to be an infinite number of infractions, each of which loosed a storm of abuse upon the offender.

Inspections have always been a time for sergeants to be picayune. But it was more than the recital of violations which upset the recruits. The inspecting NCOs accompanied their searching gazes with staccato questions: "What is the weight of your rifle, Private?" "10.42 pounds, sir." "No, Private, I mean *your* rifle with these five pounds of crud inside. When did you last wash, three years ago? What are the four life-saving steps? Where did the term 'Devildogs' come from? . . . Tell me, Private. What is this red material smiling at me from your rifle barrel? It might be paint and it might be blood. But I think it looks like *rust!* A rusty rifle will get you time in the brig and in combat it will get you killed when the sonofabitch blows up in your face!"

Some recruits knew the answers and handled the onslaughts. Others froze. "Private, when was the War of 1812 fought?" A stricken look crossed the recruit's brow. "The private doesn't know, sir." The DI himself looked incredulous for a moment, then called gleefully to his fellows that he had found "King Dummie."

The routines of boot camp continued in the evening hours. While there was still light, the drill instructors usually had the platoon out on the "grinder" practicing drill. "Free Time," the ninety minutes before Taps, was really an organized period of showers, shaves, mail call, and study, each with its own ritual. For example, to receive his mail, the recruit had to yell his name when it was called, run down the squad bay, come to attention before the drill instructor, repeat his name, clap the letter between his horizontal palms, take one step backward, shout "Aye, aye, sir!", do an about-face, and run back to his bunk. It was *not* a time to relax, and after the dialogue, exhaustion sent most directly to sleep. An emboldened few, however, might sneak into the head to write letters or talk in muffled tones.

Each night, four recruits walked two-hour fire watches up and down the 75-foot long squad bay. For once their pace and thoughts were their own. Another recruit might cry out in his sleep or an owl hoot outside. Nothing else intruded on this reverie except their own drowsiness.

Guard duty was the only other activity in all of Phase I where the recruits did anything as individuals. It wasn't exactly freedom. But there was time to reflect as they stiffly walked their lonely posts . . . until the officer of the day rounded a corner and substituted for an enemy his own verbal bombardment. "Why don't you sound off, Private?" "It is against the private's nature to yell loudly, sir." "To hell with your nature!"

The title "drill instructor" derives from his duty to teach close order drill. To the drill instructors, it is the most important subject for it demonstrates the degree to which they have instilled observable collective discipline in their recruits. It is also the only activity in which the DIs of different platoons really compete. Each DI, therefore, teaches drill in his own way, jealously guarding his secrets. He has his own accent and cadence. The DIs compete to see who can get the most complete response with the least verbal effort. Platoon 360's senior could bring the platoon to attention or set them in motion with merely a stentorian grunt from across the parade ground. Other DIs tried to imitate him and trip up the platoon but they only responded to their master's voice.

The only thing which distinguishes one platoon from the dozens of others is the guidon. This foot-square cloth with the platoon's number is the most visible symbol of the recruit's new collective identity. In the second week, the DIs used it to mark a change in their training approach. While continuing to revile individual privates' efforts, they considered the platoon sufficiently unified to humiliate *it*. "I have never seen such shitty drill," the senior said one day. "I'm embarrassed. I don't want people to know who this mob is." As they watched, he wrapped the guidon with rubber bands. On another occasion he used a different tack to shame the platoon: throwing his hat on the ground in exaggerated disgust, he cried, "You bastards all want to march in your own ways. Like a bunch of goddam mules. O.K. But there is only one mule driver in my team. On my cadence, sing out 'Hee, haw! Hee, haw'! so the whole Island can hear!"

The platoon settled into a routine after a few days, the only salient change being the above-mentioned elevation of the platoon to the place of concurrent highest loyalty and greatest contempt. But underneath the now normal level of derision, the DIs had, since Forming, been making important evaluations of the individual recruits as they came to know and type them. No matter what their frustrations and gripes were, the DIs obviously wanted the best possible platoon. This desire was a combination of both personal pride and hope for promotion. Inevitably, they decided which recruits worked hard, which were sneaks, which ones lagged (and why), and so on. To the DIs a demonstrably recalcitrant recruit was a "shitbird," and "disloyal," but most of all he was "unmotivated."

"Motivation" is stated rationale for judging a recruit's susceptibility to the Marine ethic and expectations. If a recruit is "motivated," he will present a spotless rifle for inspection. If he is "motivated," he will not "eyeball" in the chowline. If he is "motivated," he will not take the first opportunity to skylark. Because *if* he is "motivated," he

57

does not need to be told more than once or twice to "do what he is told." The "unmotivated" are punished singly or in groups: "Bends and thrusts, ready, begin!"

But PT as a punitive measure, like the extravagant language, loses some of its bite after prolonged use. Recruits who can't "get their heads and asses wired together" receive a stronger antidote.

> Motivation Platoon is assigned the mission of providing special training for recruits who because of their environmental background, acceptance of training or resistance to authority have not adjusted to the military way of life. Examples of recruits who will benefit from this program are: Those continually defiant or resentful toward authority, those pampered, overindulged or immature, those capable of success in training who repeatedly fail to perform up to their abilities . . .
>
> One Day Motivation . . . is designed to provide motivation training for the problem recruit while allowing him to remain in his original platoon . . .*

In other words, One Day Motivation is designed to make the "problem recruit" as miserable as possible. It is Receiving Barracks all over again with the physical harassment of a forced march added to the usual verbal barrages.

On a cheerless morning as rain slashed across Parris Island, 360's DIs sent eight recruits to join ninety others at One Day Motivation for a "taste of the old Corps." "You are out here because you can't square away in your own platoons. Fuck up and we keep you!" One DI immediately set off at a grueling pace, leading them around the base through every pool and gully he could find. Two other DIs rode herd imploring them with measured sarcasm, "Asshole to bellybutton! *Please* hurry up . . . *puke!*" As the recruits ran to keep up, their enveloping ponchos tripped them or the rain and their bouncing helmets blinded them and they crashed into the man in front. "Oh dear, Miss Jones. You fell, what a shame . . . *Getthefuckup!*" In the

* *Standard Operating Procedure for Recruit Training.* November 1967 M.C.R.D. Parris Island, S.C.

58

second half of their ordeal, they ran, slid, slipped, crawled and groveled through a series of foul-smelling ditches, euphemistically called an "infiltration course."

Eight abject recruits returned to their barracks in the afternoon. When other recruits snickered, they were cut short: "Best not go out there. You smell us? I'm going AWOL before I go there again. I've had mine today. I don't want anymore."

The DIs called a *post-mortem* "school circle."

These recruits were fortunate. They know what we mean about discipline. You are told exactly what is expected of you. I don't feel proud when I take a private to lock his heels in front of the C.O. One Day Motivation goes again on Friday. These privates have learned a lesson. If we have to teach you other hogs the same lesson, we will. It's up to you . . .

The recruits did not realize it but One Day Motivation was the hardest kind of disciplinary treatment they would encounter. The DIs felt that a stint at Motivation was the "last chance" for instilling the desired sense of discipline in the recruits. If that failed, the DIs would try to have the recruit set back in training.

Sundays, they rested . . . just a bit. An extra hour of sleep was one reward, church another. On the hard pews, some tried to get more sleep and had to be nudged for the hymns. Others wrote letters on the programs. Most, however, listened attentively and sang dutifully. Afterward, they washed clothes and cleaned the squad bay. But here again, minor faults aroused DI ire: "You shitbirds can live like pigs in your own homes, but in *my* barracks, you're goin' to be clean!"

The Sunday field meets were high points in Phase I. Compared to normal activities, they were fairly unstructured. DI harassment was minimal. Moreover, they gave the platoon a chance (probably unconscious) to demonstrate to the DIs and to themselves, their progress toward the new collective identity.

A field meet in Phase I gave Platoon 360 a chance to demonstrate to the DI and to themselves, their progress toward the new collective identity. The senior had based his pep talk on platoon loyalty.

You have to motivate yourselves out there. 360, not a bunch of individuals will win that field meet. We don't care if you win or lose, however, as long as you work together . . .

The meet, which consisted of different relay, sprints, push-up and pull-up contests, culminated in tugs-of-war.

Almost as if in response to their growing unity, the platoon saw another side of their senior. They saw him take off his hat, not to throw it down in disgust but to rally them. They listened dumbfoundedly when he said; "You hogs didn't do so badly today." For once, he attributed their failure to external causes. "If we hadn't been pulling on that dry road and you weren't such feathermerchants, we would have won that tug." He left no doubt that what he praised, however, was their *group* effort.

The next two weeks at the rifle range would be largely individual effort, but the recruits would never be allowed to forget that their loyalties were to platoon, Marine Corps, and country, in that order.

"Yell louder, you scummy pig!"

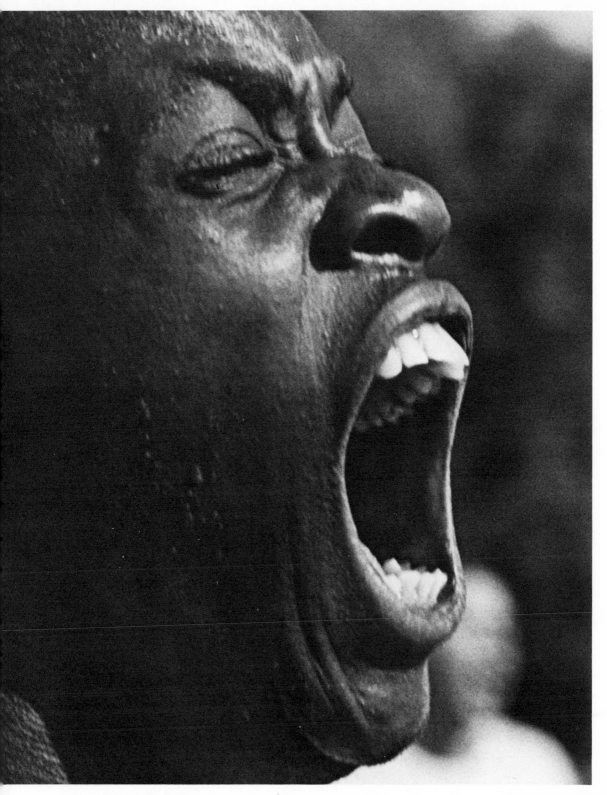

One who yelled.

Leaping for one of the bars on the Obstacle Course.

Up and . . .

. . . over?

One recruit who didn't make it
receives anything but sympathy
from the attendant DIs.

Sit-ups.

The agony with

none of the ecstasy.

After every session of PT there were runs.
Here privates help one of their lagging buddies.

**Senior DI explains
a drill movement.**

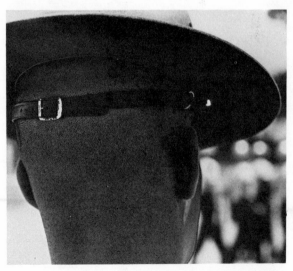

DI watches his charges.

In the early days of drill practice,
the lines are not so very straight.

DI gives unconscious body English
as his platoon marches past.

Often, commands are not heard at the rear of the
marching platoon. Confusion is the inevitable result.

A rifle familiarization class.

Even in air-conditioned classrooms, recruits get sleepy.

Inspections are used sometimes to put the recruits in one kind of shock.

"Could that just possibly be a piece of rust, you miserable scumbug?"

74

Instructor gives class in bayonet drill. **75**

"Kill!"

Pugilstick fighting is designed to teach bayonet fighting without injuring the participants.

One of the parts of the
Confidence Course is the
Slide for Life.

This private did not make it
all the way to dry land.

Climbing the A-Frame
on the Confidence
Course.

Another perspective
of that climb.

Running and crawling through
the mire, muck and mud of
One Day Motivation.

80

**Mud-covered boots halfway through
One Day Motivation.**

Dragging ammo boxes filled with sand
through a foul-smelling ditch.

This recruit has just
emerged from crawling
on his back beneath
25 yards of barbed wire.

This private has
just emerged from the ditch.

Interplatoon warfare
in the form of tugs-of-war.

84   *"Pull!"*

phase II

CHAPTER FOUR

This is my rifle. There are many like it, but this one is mine. My rifle is my best friend. It is my life . . . I must master it as I master my life.

My rifle without me is useless. Without my rifle I am useless. I must fire my rifle true. I must shoot straighter than my enemy who is trying to kill me. I must shoot him before he shoots me. I will . . .

My rifle and myself know that what counts in this war is not the rounds we fire, the noise of our burst, nor the smoke we make. We know that it is the hits that count. We will hit . . .

My rifle is human, even as I, because it is my life. Thus I will learn it as a brother. I will learn its weakness, its strength, its parts, its accessories, its sights and its barrel. I will keep my rifle clean and ready even as I am clean and ready. We will become part of each other.

We will . . .

Before God I swear this creed. My rifle and myself are the defenders of my country. We are the masters of our enemy. We are the saviors of my life.

That every Marine is a rifleman is central to the mystique of the Marine Corps. During its entire history, the Marine Corps has claimed to *be* the "grunts," the riflemen. Everyone else, from airmen to cooks, are "support elements." As if to give practical support to this article of faith, one-quarter to one-third of boot camp is devoted to the care and firing of the service rifle.

During Phase I, the drill instructors had given 360 a considerably less romanticized introduction to the weapon than the above quoted "Rifleman's Creed."

This rifle is a magazine-fed, bolt-operated, air-cooled, semi-automatic shoulder weapon. Treat it like a woman you respect. It may save your miserable life some day.

I'm sure you've all seen John Wayne movies where he kills 10,000 gooks, then slings the barrel over his shoulder and ditty-bops away. Bull shit! There's 50,000 pounds of pressure per square inch in that barrel when the bullet goes through it at 2800 feet per second. That causes friction, which causes heat, which will burn the shit out of your hands if you hold it.

Or supposed you don't like carrying ammo in cases. You want to be like Pancho Villa and wear it as a vest. I'll tell you one goddam thing. When you do that and get it wet, it corrodes and you won't be able to fire at all.

Day after day, in class and in the barracks, they cleaned, disassembled and reassembled their rifles. The rifle's cycle of functioning became part of the nightly "dialogue." "*Feeding, Chambering, Locking, Firing, Unlocking, Extraction, Ejection, Cocking.*"

Before dawn, their fifth Saturday on Parris Island, Platoon 360 marched a mile to new barracks near the Rifle Range. Upon arrival, they received new equipment—shooting jackets, score books, bullet magazines, and other paraphernalia. They would have a different SOP (days beginning and ending an hour earlier to make maximum use of morning light and calm). All their attention was to be concentrated on rifle marksmanship. The change in location also signaled a change in treatment.

The range is where we work first as individuals and second as a platoon. This is the only time you will have a chance to show pride in yourselves. These two weeks will be the most fun at boot camp. There is nothing like the feeling of watching them raise a white spotter to mark a bull's eye. You have no reason to be afraid of this weapon. Each of you pigs weighs from 130 to 200 pounds. The rifle weighs 11½ and the thing that kills you comes out the other end.

Getting into the firing position is painful. We won't lie to you. It takes discipline. This is where you show how much you can do by yourselves. But don't fuck off . . . we know all the tricks. *We* were privates once.

The Rifle Range had its own set of physical and verbal rituals. The first, longest, and most agonizing was the seven days spent "on the grass," learning the four firing positions—prone, sitting, kneeling, and offhand (standing). Despite what the drill instructors had said, all seemed to be special torments to no readily apparent end. Beneath their jackets, and sweat shirts, the privates itched and sweated. Stabs of pain announced the discovery of new muscles. The sun grew hotter and the ground harder. Rifle slings bit deeper into their arms. The sweat stung and clouded their vision. There was no excitement in firing empty rifles. The drill instructors paced up and down the lines of squirming recruits.

But in spite of the continuing tattoo of harassment and ridicule, the recruits watched another change in the drill instructors. Instead of repeating the now well-known phrases of contempt and scorn and letting it go at that, they took several privates having the most difficulty "snapping-in" and formed them into a "Sniper Team." The senior spent all of his time with them and by the end of the week, they held better positions than the rest of the platoon. He was obviously proud when he paraded them before the others to demonstrate their new skill.

Respites of sorts came during classes in a teaching shed nearby, where, interspersed with pungent lectures by the PMI (Primary Marksmanship Instructor), they intoned a new set of reminders.

> Mechanical zero is when the long line on the moveable base is lined up with the long line on the stationary base . . .
> Sight alignment is when the tip of the front sight blade is halfway up and centered from left to right in the rear sight aperture . . .
> One click of elevation moves the strike of the bullet one inch on the target for every 100 yards of range . . .

But there was little rest for the aching. The rifle holding exercises continued in the barracks. "The more you sweat in peace, the less you bleed in war," an anonymous masochist had written inside one private's locker box.

Platoon 360's first chance to *fire* any weapons came late in the first week.

> We're going to fire the .45 pistol. There will be one coach for each private. It's too easy to wave that weapon around. Don't any of you privates get the idea of zapping your DI, or PMI. We'll be fifty yards away behind wire, mines, bunkers, and sentry dogs.
> On the other hand, if you want to commit suicide, we'll give you a place all by yourself. Just make like you're aiming in, and put the muzzle under your chin. But strip first. We don't want you fucking up Marine Corps gear.

There was no attempt to teach pistol marksmanship, only familiarization. (The pistols had been used so much, they wouldn't fire straight anyway.)

Even the drill instructors realized that the first week at the range was boring, if necessary work and tried to relieve the monotony in several ways. They expanded the list of nicknames: John the Baptist, Daffy Duck, Rodent, Guppy Smile, Psycho, Coke Bottles, the last a reference to the private's thick glasses. During the hottest part of the

90

day, the series DIs organized arm wrestling contests between their platoons with extra cigarettes as prizes.

At the end of the squad bay, they hung up a bulletin board, which became the "Hog Board." The drill instructors had told the platoon during Phase I to write home for "pictures of your girlfriends and wives in the most revealing poses short of outright porno." They were warned not to "embarrass us by getting picture of 'scags'." That mock threat suggested that the Hog Board was primarily for the amusement and prestige of the drill instructors. But it gave some diversion to the privates as well.

At other times the high jinks were spontaneous, a product of individual drill instructors' imaginations. A toad found in the squad bay, became Drill Instructor Toad, and one private his trainer. When it died for inexplicable reasons, the private received a stern reprimand and the toad was given a burial with "full military honors." Another private who had been a Baptist minister, read the service:

> We are gathered here on this solemn occasion to mourn the passing of Drill Instructor Toad. The Lord giveth and the Lord taketh away. Blessed be the name of the Lord.

The entire platoon filed slowly past the coffin (a black soap dish) and the toad was lowered into the deep . . . commode.

At the end of the first week, they fired their rifles for the first time. The ten rounds fired on the 900-inch line gave the instructors groups of hits so that they might suggest improvements in position and technique. It was a *pro forma* training exercise, but the PMI followed the platoon back to its barracks with the parting remark to his fellows, "I guess I'll go harass the troops." Brandishing the targets, he said:

> You people are something else! Afraid of that weapon? Twenty-three yards away and some of you can't hit the fucking target!
>
> Look at this shit! Piss poor sight-alignment, piss poor spot weld, piss poor trigger squeeze, hell, no squeeze at all, jerking, bucking,

chasing the bull's eye. You haven't learned a fucking thing all week. That's what we get for going easy on you . . .

The platoon had not done as badly as the PMI declared nor as well as the DIs had hoped. But those possibilities could never be conceded outright. On the contrary, the senior rose and stalked away, saying he had "never seen such a performance." The recruits did not know it was his day off, anway. *They* spend the weekend in purgatory, washing clothes, cleaning rifles and, of course, "snapping-in."

But Monday was different. Instead of stopping at the class shed, they marched through the moist darkness toward the "Big Line," pausing only briefly to pick up heavy green boxes of ammunition. One-third of the platoon peeled off and disappeared. They would "pull" and mark targets for the other two-thirds, then fire later in the morning. The platoon reached a small rise and halted. Over their right shoulders the eastern blackness began to crack apart with streaks of purple and blue. Two hundred yards away the growing light carved out a row of 50 six-foot square targets.

Each day they would fire for Qualification, which meant scoring at least 190 out of a possible 250 points. At the 200 yard-line they had 10 rounds slow fire in the standing position (12 minutes), and 10 rounds rapid fire sitting (60 seconds). From 300 yards, they fired 5 rounds sitting and 5 rounds kneeling (slow fire), and 10 rounds prone (rapid fire). Finally, 10 rounds prone at the 500-yard line (slow fire).

During the week of firing, a coach is assigned to every two privates. He checks their position, helps them get the correct "dope" on their rifles and make sure they do not step off the firing line with loaded rifles . . . Except for the drill instructors, the coaches are the only boot camp personnel with whom the recruits have extended contact. They vary widely in manner in which they relate to the recruits. Most do their job with little interest and less fanfare. A small number act like frustrated drill instructors, alternately ignoring and scorning the recruits' efforts. At the opposite extreme, an equally small number become extremely involved with the recruits and suffer or exalt depending upon how their students fire.

Through the morning, almost the only sounds were insistent me-

92

tallic puffs as thousands of rounds left hundreds of rifles. The slow fire, even when the entire series was firing, sounded interminable. The rapid fire has a desperate convulsive quality. The only other sound was the droning voice of the NCO in charge with his periodic messages like, "Cease fire, Cease fire. Unload, clear, and lock your weapons. When they have been checked by the coach, you may stand up. Next relay . . ."

Few members of Platoon 360 qualified that first day, Nor were they expected to. Giving them even that much comfort, however, would have been heresy for the DIs.

Undoubtedly you set a record out there today! You fucked over these weapons so much they probably will never fire again for other privates. You disgraced them. Everything you possibly could have done wrong, you did.

Your coaches couldn't believe it. You went spastic. Are you pissed off at us or the PMI? At least half of you assholes forgot to put dope on your rifles. Numb nuts Harper was firing on BOTH targets during slow fire.

Thank God we're not going to Vietnam with you creeps. We'll sit back here and read your death notices in the Navy Times.

NEVER has there been a Monday like this one. Of course, dearies, writing letters at night is more important than thinking about marksmanship . . . You'd better learn to pray.

Throughout the rest of the week they worked hard. Bit by bit they brought up their scores. The tension increased. It would be close, whether they all improved enough to reach 190. One private had particular difficulty. Again and again he fired—3s, 2s, zeros. His rifle barrel grew hot from firing extra rounds. After one gruesome string, he burst into tears. He told the drill instructors he had not wanted to come into the Marine Corps. His father had been killed in Korea, two brothers had died and one had been wounded in Vietnam. Their only reply was "Wouldn't you like to get the bastards who killed your brothers?" But after the private had left, one DI said to the other, "He

93

shouldn't be here. I'll bet his goddam relatives pressured him into joining and he's scared stiff."

On Record Day eve, it was "all over but the praying. You can break out any religious hardware you might have. Some of you bastards will need all the help you can get." The series was taken to a movie full of adventure, heroics and escape. After Taps, the senior read passages from Marine Corps history and talked to them quietly:

> You are the bearers of the proudest military tradition in the world. That tradition was built upon discipline and rifle marksmanship. Qualification tomorrow is the first step in joining that tradition. To go "unq" is to betray both yourselves and the Marine Corps.
>
> Get some sleep, get up and be ready to fire that rifle. The PMI and drill instructors can get shook but you cannot and will not . . .

The next morning they got to the range a little earlier than usual. Only the DIs' cigarettes and the sputtering carbon lamps (to reduce glare on rifle sights) cut the darkness. Some fired better than they had all week. Others shot worse. Some forgot to put the "dope" on their weapons. Several fired on the wrong targets. By noon it was apparent that 360 had done below average, though not as abysmally as they were told. Nevertheless, the senior was genuinely depressed and when he spoke, obscenities were conspicuous by their absence:

> Don't look down, especially you "unqs." Hold your heads up. You should be proud. It took real effort to drop thirteen out of seventy-five. We had faith and you stabbed us in the back. Now I know what they mean when they say 'Never trust a private. He'll betray you every time.' Sergeant Thomas, get them out of my sight.

It was the gloomiest afternoon of boot camp as they turned in their equipment, cleaned their rifles, and changed barracks.

But for both groups of antagonists, it was neither the end of the

94

world nor of training. The DIs had to prepare for Phase III and the recruits put in a week on mess duty. It was an incredibly active and sweaty hiatus in the training cycle. Each day the platoon worked sixteen hours in the sculleries, potshops, gallies, and storerooms serving 1600 other recruits. There was time to savor the success or deaden the failure on the range and the opportunity (if not the permission) to talk to one another. By the end of the week, however, they were ready to return to training.

Ungrammatical but crystal-clear vow on the blackboard of a teaching shed at the Rifle Range.

Looking down the business end
of an M-14 rifle.

"Get your back down!"
Drill instructor gives recruit
extra help in learning
the prone position.

Drill instructor gets down in horizontal position to see
if private has rifle sights properly aligned.

Drill instructor tries to move rifle barrel to see if
private has a firm enough grip on the weapon.
(This was during snapping-in, *not* live firing.)

During free moments in the
barracks, the drill instructors had the platoon study
their notes in this position
in order to stretch the
muscles which would be used
most when firing from the
sitting position.

While the rest of the platoon
goes for a water break,
two rifle instructors
work on with a member of
the "Sniper Team."
Other privates' rifles in
the foreground.

101

Another use of spare time in the barracks. All recruits hold their rifles in the off-hand position with one arm so as to strengthen their arm muscles.

Arm wrestling between members of different platoons provided a measure of relaxation and good-natured competition during the noon hours.

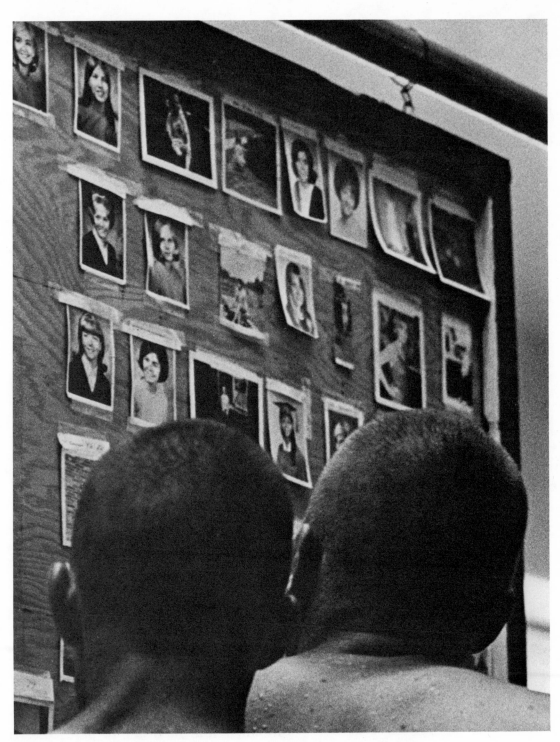

The Hog Board, to be "covered with the most revealing
pictures of girl friends, wives, and sisters, short of outright
pornography." Very few took up the challenge and offered
instead normal high school graduation pictures.

"Ready on the Left,
Ready on the Right,
Ready on the Firing Line!
Watch your targets!"

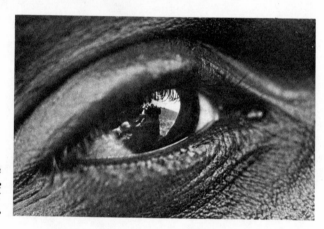

Rifle's rear sight and part of the
range reflected in the eyeball of
one private.

An entire 75-man platoon firing at once on the
900-inch line in order to get a feel for their
rifles prior to moving over to the "Big Line."

Spent cartridge leaps up and rifle recoils
back into private's shoulder.

Private waits at the 200-yard line for enough light by which to fire.

Rifle coaches vary widely in the degree of involvement with recruits. This one rejoiced and suffered with his charges as if they were his own kin.

From the 300-yard line, each recruit fires five rounds
sitting and five kneeling.

One recruit who did not qualify
gets some comfort from two drill instructors.

Coffee by the gallon.

Hot, sweaty, endless work
in the potshop.

More sweaty work,
cleaning the floors of the
scullery in the mess hall.

Entry of recruits into serving line at the mess hall.

The hours of mess duty are so long and exhausting, that the recruits "pulling" mess duty grab every moment, even their own mess time, to pull soggy letters out of back pockets and read them.

phase III

CHAPTER FIVE

FROM mess duty, Platoon 360 almost literally jumped into the pool for classes in Water Survival. Drown Proofing, as it was also known, taught the recruits how to remain motionless in the water for periods up to several hours, using their clothing as floats. It required discipline for anyone, let alone fearful eighteen-year-olds, to master this technique. But after some anxious moments and verbal prodding by the instructors ("Go ahead, drown, you coward!"), they learned the trick. The nonswimmers, meanwhile, received lessons at the other end of the pool.

Myriad activities like Drown Proofing, drill, exams, and preparations for graduation combined to make Phase III simultaneously the most active and the calmest period of boot camp. The very press of concluding training left the drill instructors little or no time to "harass the troops," even if they believed it necessary. In effect they said, "Show us how good a *platoon* you have become." Phase III was, therefore, a summing-up, a fusion of all previous objective and subjective training.

The main motivational tool is the threat of setting an individual recruit back in training. It rarely happens this late in training, a fact which embitters some DIs. "Put 'em on the bus. That's our job." This inner frustration that some recruits may graduate without proper discipline is perhaps best summed up in a phrase of ultimate scorn for their own authority: "Fuck you, Sarge!" However, the recruits don't recognize this expression as out of the ordinary and the dark vision of a setback probably works simply because they are so near the end of training.

The Marine Corps, more than any other service, prides itself on appearance. Since the DIs epitomized this pride and since their job was, after all, to remake the recruits in their own image, they paid particularly close attention to the outfitting of their recruits. A full day was spent getting the last of four uniform fittings.

There was no formal PT during Phase III. But the platoon got plenty of physical exercise on morning runs and in hand-to-hand combat classes. Gallows humor reminiscent of the bayonet classes characterized the latter:

> Suppose you're running down the trail and suddenly you're face to face with Charlie but you ain't got a weapon. I'm telling you your natural weapons: the meaty portion of your hand, the fingers as gouges, the knees, elbows, or even spit in his face . . .
>
> Where is he vulnerable? Just about everywhere—his eyes, face, neck, solar plexus, kidneys and of course the groin—I don't care if he's white, purple, Chinese, French, Russian or Hindu, he wants to protect those jewels and that's your opportunity to strike him in another vital spot . . .

The platoon won another streamer by successfully running the Physical Readiness Test (PRT). It consisted of (1) an assault course, (2) rope climb, (3) fireman's carry rescue, and (4) a three-mile forced march within a prescribed time period. The DI's only comment was a sidelong, "Well, at least you won't be a purple mob, after all."

One morning in the last week, the series marched five miles to the other side of the Island, to Elliott's Beach for practical application tests on the material they had learned in boot camp. For the first time, they dressed like Marines, exchanging their "chrome domes" for steel helmets and donning "light marching packs." At the Beach, they pitched tents and ate C-rations. There was an air of anticipation now. The end of their ordeal seemed nearer than ever before.

116

The testing lasted most of the afternoon. They bound imaginary wounds, showed their prowess with bayonets, demonstrated military "customs and courtesies," and disassembled rifles blindfolded. The DIs had to remain in the tent area. Outwardly calm, they smoked incessantly as they counted the return of each successful private. The results were more important to them than they let on for they had been largely responsible for teaching this material. If all the recruits passed, it meant another streamer and an additional boost in platoon unity and morale. When the last recruit came back suppressing an unmilitary grin, the DIs ceremoniously added the new streamer and permitted the platoon a few moments pandemonium. "They're really together now!" said one. Then quickly he growled, "Back in ranks, mob!" and marched them to chow.

That evening Platoon 360 joined in a significant ritual. The DIs gave them permission and encouragement to improvise skits and monologues about their experiences in boot camp. They hesitated, like small children approaching an elephant for the first time. Gingerly they recalled their own foibles and *faux pas*. Growing bolder, they began to lampoon some DI characteristics. No retribution ensued and for the next hour, nothing was sacred. One private gave a marvelous imitation of a junior DI dressing down a much larger recruit. He even succeeded in capturing the DI's particularly dry insinuating tone. Another private demonstrated how he imagined a DI would act in civilian situations such as of a baseball game, in a supermarket or just taking a shower "at my cadence." Like good children, the recruits were even permitted to remain up past Taps. Implicit in this satiric exchange of roles was the DIs' belief that their control over the recruits would be greater after such a release.

It was.

Following this "night in the field," the series marched back to their mainside barracks. They barely had time to clean their rifles, boots and selves before the intra-series drill competition. For the recruits, "drill comp" was the culmination of hours and hours on the "grinder," possibly another streamer, but little else. For the DIs, it was almost the climax of training. Throughout it all they had tried to "psyche out" each other about the progress and proficiency of their own

117

platoon's marching. A team of senior NCOs would now judge each platoon on the precision with which it performed a specific series of drill movements.

The formal verdict came dispassionately. The informal judging conducted across the parade field by each senior's peers showed its sarcasm and minutiae how seriously the drill instructors took their titles.

Although 360 did not win, the accustomed torrent of abuse did not come. By this time, there were just too many activities and the DIs felt this tactic would no longer affect platoon unity one way or the other.

There were almost daily inspections now. To prepare for them the platoon spent long hours inside and outside the barracks polishing, scraping, cutting, measuring, buffing, and wiping. All those odd implements they had been issued at Receiving found purposes. The Q-tips, toothbrushes, paint brushes and pipe cleaners went into action against the forces of dust and rust.

The day before the final (Command) inspection was one of organized chaos. The platoon cleaned their gear in unison: 45 minutes on belts, 30 minutes on buckles, 45 minutes for showers, etc. The DIs checked rifles, every item of clothing, every piece of gear, keeping up a steady stream of banter to break the tedium: "Look at that private's head! It's so misshapen, you couldn't sell it in a cheap melon store!" After a final check, the rifles were bedded down between cleaner sheets than those the recruits had! Spotless uniforms were hung on long racks. Taps sounded before the recruits finished shining their shoes, so they took turns in the head completing this final task.

The drill instructors woke them ten minutes early the next morning to beat the rest of the series to chow. After wolfing down their meal, the platoon raced back to the barracks for final preparations. They dressed with the care of bullfighters. As if on eggs, they walked outside, fearful of damaging the fragile crease in their trousers or the spitshine on their shoes. Breathlessly, they inspected their rifles in the morning light. Was there any rust? Had they shaved close enough? Did they remember their rifle numbers?

They would soon know. It took two hours for the inspecting officers

118

and NCOs to complete this the most exacting of all Marine inspections. They didn't "go spastic" or shout as their practiced eyes surveyed each recruit. A faulty tie, here, ill-shined shoes there, a poor shave, dust on the front sight. The scratch of pencils recording these violations and the triple trump of rifles being brought to "inspection arms" were the only sounds. Finally, they drew away from the last recruit and conferred with the DIs. The platoon knew that if they passed, training was over.

They remained in suspense until the platoon photograph was taken—they were home free.

That afternoon after the platoon had turned in its equipment, those privates whose families had come for their graduation, were given four hours' liberty with them.

The graduation ceremony the next day lasted only thirty minutes. The series "passed in review" before the awed and admiring spectators. The 3rd Battalion commander presented marksmanship and platoon "honorman" awards to individual privates. He was "pleased to be the first person to address them as Marines." At rigid attention, they received the command "360 Series, Fallout!" In unison, three hundred newly christened Marines did an about-face, gave a thunderous "Aye, aye, sir!" and exploded in all directions. They were on base liberty. Some ran to their families. Others lined up for phone calls home. Later, these tan, ramrod straight young men explored the Island, parts of which were burned into their memories and parts completely unknown. Unconsciously they fell in step with each other but couldn't match the ambling civilian pace of their families.

At one time or other, nearly all the recruits stopped at one of the Depot restaurants or snack shops where Boot Camp seemed to be the only topic of conversation. These *post-mortems* were made amidst the gorging of formerly forbidden foods. The tables groaned beneath hamburgers, Cokes, and candy, and the ashtrays overflowed with the new freedom.

Some were unrepentant to the end. They had fought the system throughout training. "This shit was too much. I will never learn to be a killer." A second group, who, while not enthusiastic about the training, or the mystique, had learned to "play the game." "The drill

119

instructors had a job to do." "The senior was OK, but those juniors were real bastards." "You can't beat the system, anyway."

But most felt that boot camp had been "good for us." "Now I see that if the things in civilian life really mean anything to me, I ought to be ready to die for them." "I used to be a street-corner bum. Now I feel part of something larger than myself." Unconsciously they had adopted the DIs' frame of reference and even language. "If only we could have squared away that 10 per cent who were always fucking up the platoon, we would have been outstanding." They criticized just those individuals who in civilian life they would have admired for their independence and "coolness."

Of course the recruits were glad to be out. But simultaneously, they had come to believe that their survival at boot camp resulted more from the Marine Corps' benevolent paternalism than from their own abilities. They felt grateful to the drill instructors for pushing them beyond what they had considered their limits and giving them "something to believe in." The harassment, sweat, scorn and ridicule had a purpose, they now *believed*.

The negative had become positive. And the Marine Corps had another set of converts.

Base liberty was a temporary freedom . . . The platoon had to be back in the barracks by 1900. They said goodbye to their families and began packing seabags for their departure the next morning. Just before Taps, the senior gathered the platoon together for a final "school circle." He read out the orders, the Military Occupational Specialty for each private.

Dupre—0100, a fucking clerk; Connor, Ringler—1800, Engineers, you go out and find mines; 0200, Intelligence, none of you cocksuckers are smart enough for that; Martinez, Gautz, 2500 Communications—that means you'll probably carry a radio on your backs.

And so on down the line. More than half were 0300s—Rifleman. He stopped in the middle of reading the names. "Don't let me hear any more sucking of breath . . . 0300 *is* the Marine Corps!" When he had finished, his voice lost its stentorian quality.

Instant willing obedience to orders. That's all we tried to teach you down here. Some of you learned it. Others didn't. It's sad when people who were volunteers don't have the guts to stick it out. I've seen 100 percent draftee platoons who did better than you. But bad as you were, you weren't the worst to come through this place.

The Marine Corps is without doubt the finest fighting organization in the world. It was built on discipline. Discipline is not just marching in step or keeping your mouth shut. It's what gets you out of a hole when lead is flying around. By no means will you like what you have to do. If we had a choice, we would not be in Vietnam. But it's our job.

Work as hard as you can. Don't suck ass. Be yourself. You are an ambassador of the United States and the Marine Corps. Good luck.

The next morning they boarded buses identical to those which had brought them to Parris Island ten long weeks before. The DIs spoke jokingly and even affectionately to a few individuals. But it was so novel and out of character that the privates seemed embarrassed. No one waved in either direction as the buses pulled away in clouds of acrid blue exhaust, carrying these young men a step closer to war.

Slowly, quietly, each man lost in his own individual thoughts, the drill instructors walked back into the deserted barracks. They finished their coffee, smoked another cigarette and prepared to go back to Receiving for 75 more recruits . . .

Instructor demonstrates how to
defend oneself unarmed against an
opponent with a bayonet.

Instructor lets loose with a
couple of pulled punches to
show various ways of
demolishing one's opponent
when the latter has
no weapons.

122

A variation on unarmed
combat—one recruit
with pugilstick and
the other without,
square off.

Recruits run through series of
obstacles to practice knife attack
movements, but, even here, they
are not free of the drill
instructors' barbed commentary.

125

Platoon marches past
early morning rain
puddle on way to
Elliott's Beach.

The one time at boot camp when
recruits can satirize their
experiences. Some of them did
magnificent characterizations
of drill instructors dressing
down recruits.

As the recruits prepared for
their final examinations, the
drill instructors permitted
them to study in small groups.

**Drill Competition
—the climax
of those long
hours on the hot
gravel parade fields.**

One of the judges at drill competition, a sergeant major, watches one of the platoons march past. Meanwhile, the drill instructors of other platoons in the competition stand by doing their own judging.

Preparations for their last test—
final field inspection. They "strip"
the rifle down completely, then clean
every piece over and over again,
as in applying Q-tips to
the flash suppressor.

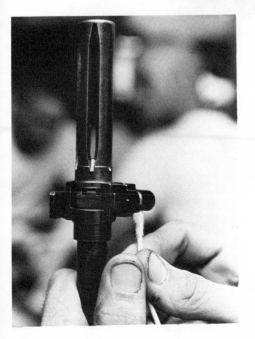

133

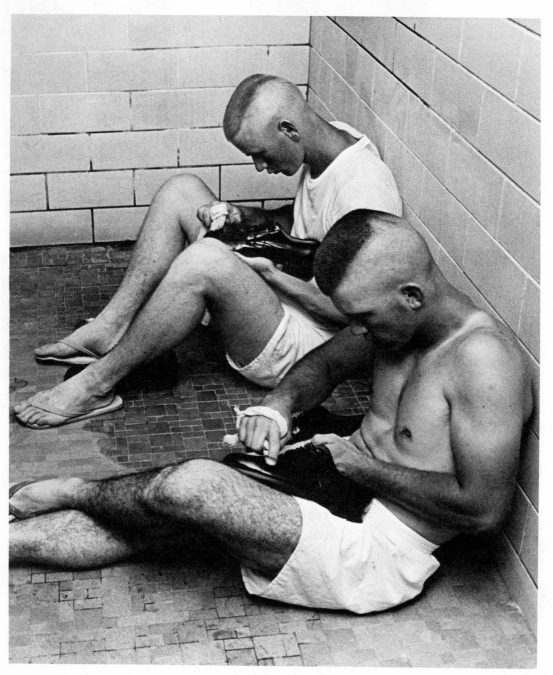

When they get a chance, some sneak
into the shower to put the finishing
touches on their shoes.

Finally all the rifles
are clean to the drill
instructors' satisfaction
and they are literally
bedded down for the night.

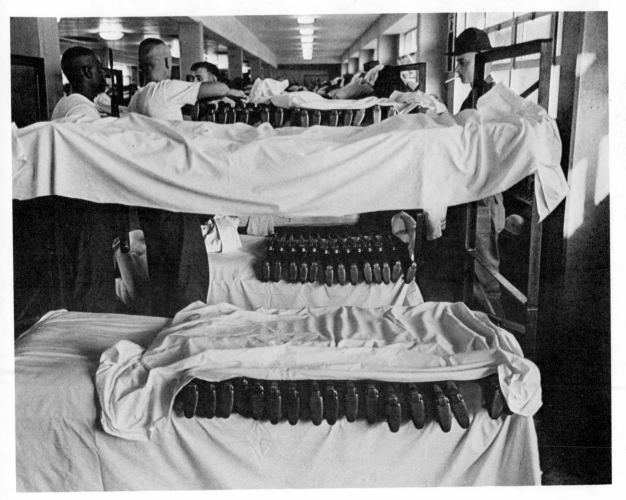

One NCO checks each private while a drill
instructor stands by to record violations.

The platoon picture.
Drill instructors could not resist
hamming for the base photographer.

Platoon passes in review before families and friends on Graduation Day.

138

Platoon 360.

A proud family
congratulates their boy.
At least nominally he
is no longer a recruit;
he is a Marine.

The next morning,
the series (240 men) boarded buses
for Camp Lejeune, North Carolina,
for more training . . . and the war.